www.finishinglinepress.com

The Sea is My Ugly Twin

poems by

Marcella Remund

Finishing Line Press
Georgetown, Kentucky

The Sea is My Ugly Twin

*To Allen, Jesse, Ryan, Dulce, Max, Mom, Dad, Dan, Mike, Joe,
the Women Poets Collective, and all my Verm and beyond Sisters,
for a deep, beautiful OCEAN of love & support.*

ACKNOWLEDGMENTS

My gratitude to these journals and their editors for publishing the following
poems:

Amethyst Arsenic, "The Sea is My Ugly Twin"
The Briar Cliff Review, "Drought"
Pacific Review, "Lugubrious Monsters"
Pasque Petals, "Lunar," "Seagulls in the Parking Lot"
all the universe shining, Scurfpea Publishing Anthology, "Hermitage,"
    "Turtle"

Publisher: Leah Maines
Editor: Christen Kincaid
Cover Art: Joe Prescher www.joeprescher.com
Author Photo: Marcella Remund
Cover Design: Elizabeth Maines McCleavy

Printed in the USA on acid-free paper.
Order online: www.finishinglinepress.com
            also available on amazon.com

Author inquiries and mail orders:
Finishing Line Press
P. O. Box 1626
Georgetown, Kentucky 40324
U. S. A.

Table of Contents

The Sea is My Ugly Twin 1

The Boy Who Practiced Drowning 2

Lugubrious Monsters 3

Turtle 5

Why in This Metaphor, I Am the Irish God Manannán
    Mac Lir, and not His Daughter, Niamh 6

Pretty Sister's Visit 7

Seagulls in the Parking Lot.. 8

Hermitage 9

Halcyon... 11

Lunar 12

Mother Sea's Lament 13

Slipstream 14

Turista 15

Blue Gardenia 16

Narcissi... 17

St. Elmo.. 18

To My Lgbtq2, Straight, and Corporate
    Friends, in Terms of Sea Creatures 19

South Dakota Water: A True Love Story............................... 20

Prehensile Aquatic.. 21

Triton's Daughter Sneaks Out at Night 22

Water to Dust... 23

What He Tried to Tell You.. 24

St. Eulalia of Merida... 25

Drought... 26

Tin Girl 27

Wild Blue Yonder 28

THE SEA IS MY UGLY TWIN

We were not born, nor formed, nor fashioned from a lump of clay, a rib bone, the condensation of breath. She and I—translucent split cell of hydrogen infused with oxygen and a soup of salts, sparked by something (does it matter what?), clinging to one another—simply came to be. I crept onto land, grew arms and legs, shut my gills, crawled off after a mate. I shriveled to the size of a hairless monkey in the drying sun, until the only mate I could find was another dried up nugget. We hobbled into the shade and made our animal noises.

My ugly sister gets all the attention: her wispy, green-gold hair and its wreath of shells, the undulations of her embrace, her liquid skin. The moon pulls at her, slips between her scales. She has that weepy look in her eyes, those black puddles. Herself/sea/moon/salt is her mate. She is mother and father, infant and dispersing crone, drifting egg and sperm. And why *wouldn't* they all want her? She fits into every crevice, soothes every sting, softens and reshapes the crags and rock ledges, washes away whatever dirt the beautiful animals drag in.

THE BOY WHO PRACTICED DROWNING

He was always long gone by the time
I threw the life preserver, not even
a bubble breaking at the surface.

I pictured him standing stock-still
on the bottom, silt between his toes,
his grey eyes blinkblinkblinking.

Later, I would see him dried out
at the hardware store, buying
three-penny nails for his drunk old man

or getting pummeled by Spider
behind the Seat 'N Eat,
his fishbone legs akimbo,

or at the 66 buying cigarettes
and a paper for his shut-in mom,
and that nickel pack of sun seeds

he'd spit all the way home. Next
day, I'd skid down the dock
like sliding into home, throw the ring

a split second too late. I'd imagine
billowing silt again, his pale eyes,
blonde hair drifting like chara

in the soupy green water.
Brother, that crazy boy
sure knew how to drown.

LUGUBRIOUS MONSTERS

> *...lugubrious monsters made of sea foam, mermaids with*
> *fishy private parts...* —Anthony Doerr

You can't placate lugubrious monsters.
In their stubborn, dismal drudgery,
they refuse to be happy, satisfied,
or even slightly less harumphy.

Who wouldn't be all sobs and misery,
to be only a wisp under a bed, a moan
in a closet, a sudden, nostalgic odor
any open window can waft away?

Lugubrious monsters come in many shapes:
sirens, medusas, churels, pig women,
norns, teenage girls, housewives, divorcees,
grandmothers left in cold dayrooms.

Here by the sea, you want mermaids.
You forget cloaca, that solitary, fishy gate
through which all things must pass: feces,
urine, your romantic misconceptions.

And when she doesn't match the starlit
fairytale you imagine in bed,
when the sheets are full of barnacles,
the room smells like candles and squid ink,

when she's run a line of slimy algae down
your spine with fingers meant to gut fish,
when you ask her to sing and she barks
like a kelpie, when sucker fish gasp

and flop on your pillow, when she grins
her pointy yellow teeth at you, when
her barbed fins cut your legs to ribbons,
how fast the lights come on! How fast

you leave her high and dry! So who can blame
lugubrious monsters for weeping sounds
in the dark, for telltale odors, for hiding
in closets, behind the dust and myths?

In my dream of the turtle,
she lumbers out of the water
onto a gravel road. I'm on the other
side in the trees, watching for cars.
She's deliberate, old, the size
of a puddle or a boggy fairy ring.
I can't stop her from crossing.

In your dream of the turtle,
her shell is missing, she's on her back.
You're holding her in one hand
as she struggles to right herself.
She's young, wet and smooth,
the size of your open palm.
You're searching for her shell.

We both dream the turtle
on the night before the burial.
Maybe the Taoists are right—
the turtle is all of us (she, you, me).
She is sky, sea, the link between.
She is prehistoric, premonitory, old,
young, our sign that life carries on.

WHY IN THIS METAPHOR, I AM THE IRISH GOD MANANNÁN MAC LIR, AND NOT HIS DAUGHTER, NIAMH

Niamh's story goes like this:
Maiden with golden hair, face so fair,
body of a god's daughter, blahblahblah.

She falls in love with the poet Oisín,
and the rest is all Oisín this, Oisín that,
blahblahblah.

But her father, Manannán mac Lir!
He cloaks his friends in ocean mist,
keeps them safe, invisible.

His horse *Enbarr* canters atop waves
as if the sea were prairie. Manannán's
cauldron of rebirth makes him Guardian

of *Mag Mell*, the Otherworld,
where no sickness, death, or decay
takes hold. Daily, he feasts

on yesterday's reborn swine.
His sword cuts through rock,
forces truth from his enemies.

He is trickster, master of disguise,
wearer of the flaming helmet, bearer
of the silver apple branch, loyal ally.

And oh! If all this weren't enough,
his grief is so great it swells
into rivers that run to the sea.

PRETTY SISTER'S VISIT

I bring my lover, my sweet pruned nugget, to the edge of the water, dooryard of my childhood home, so desperate am I to drink in once more that sustaining soup. Nugget wants to wait for dark, but it won't help—my ugly sister Sea lives so comfortably with murk. So of course she finds us, our odor of dust, our pulse of warm blood. She likes us blind and groping, I guess, the way she salts our eyes, shuts our drying lungs, blindfolds us with slippery kelp. Not satisfied that her beautiful sister is already split-finned, scaleless and brittle, she must silence me too, stop me from plucking her seastars, from snapping off the coral, from wearing her clothes.

SEAGULLS IN THE PARKING LOT

Seagulls in the parking lot at Coffee Cup,
off I-29 in northern South Dakota, seem out
of place, paradoxical. There's no ocean here,

unless you count the lapping waves of corn
& beans, the whitecaps of drying wheat. No fish
either, so parking lot gulls hunt paper cups.

There's no sand here, either, just the gravel
of glass and ground shell, stowaways in tire tread
from wetter places. There's no ocean here.

This is promising frontier though, so flighty
seagulls follow spit chew and burger wrappers
to the ditch-dry parking lot at the Coffee Cup.

These rogue gulls, their unflapping sail-wings,
their sextant eyes and webbed feet, call and circle,
displaced over asphalt and oceanless prairie.

In my landlocked dreams, gulls wing along
a shore, spearing smelt or beaking turtle eggs.
I'm in a turtleneck, in a palm hut near the ocean.
Crabs on a reed grass mat claw toward my coffee cup.

HERMITAGE

Day 1.

You can't breathe. In the stillness, terror.
Like a flock of birds, you trust noise.

You hear each rapid *ka-thump* of your heart.
It makes you cry, shiver, imagine dying.

You don't unpack. You study a road map, look
for a busy corner where you could hide.

You plan your story: *Yes, it was pleasant
and all, but really, who needs it?*

You play your iPod till the batteries go.
A spider weaves. You try to sleep.

Day 2.

You make coffee, stand in the doorway,
one foot on the threshold. Grey rabbit
crouches under sumac.

Midmorning, your teeth unclench,
shoulders drop. You sweep, dust, arrange
pen, paper, teacup & spoon

on the cabin table, like a map. You stare
at the lake—ripples, rings, oil slick
on the green-black deep.

Time lets you go. You sit on the crumbling dock,
watch swallows dip and skim,
dip and skim, as if that's all.

Day 3.

Before dawn, you walk to the water, each step
threading you to earth's core. You sing Shaker

hymns. Songs come back across the water,
echoed, altered. You write about halcyon's nest.

Diurnal instinct lulls you into unfurled sleep
at dusk, your breathing deep as a lake.

Map of cabin, water, valley, sky, stillness
imprint on your dreams.

Day 4.

Wind frills a still lake's
glass into etched scallops,
beads of turtle snout.

Today's map unfolds—
flycatcher wing, frog rumble,
long cattail shadows.

Day 5.

Light, water, map, silence

HALCYON

Midwinter, when the night goes on forever, Alcyone the kingfisher comes to the shore, calls to Ceyx, her beloved. Daughter of the wind and son of the morning star, they cobble together mud, roots, and blue feathers, set sail aboard their makeshift raft. Their only provision, a grassy cup of white eggs. For a few windless days they float, feed each other speared fish and hapless swallows, her father Aeolus soothing the sea to calm.

Maybe that's all we get: a brief interval when we aren't buffeted, a truce in which to catch a breath, feather a nest, lay eggs. Maybe turbulence is our nature, and we are meant to be buoyed about, encrusted with barnacles, dashed on the rocks. Maybe we are meant to be food for what lurks beneath the waves. Maybe we are anchored only by regret and foreboding. But is it so much to ask, Aeolus, for just a few more days of settled seas?

LUNAR

September moon is yin and yang,
light and shadow, rock and water.

Both *Rahu* and *Ketu*, she strings me
along by a tide of veins,

her silver eye demure, hidden
behind a dark and half-closed lid.

Or she stirs me to flame, wide
unblinking eye like a hunting cat's,

prism fixed and burning her silver
into my breast, lotus aflame.

Some sleepless nights, she calls
me to pirouette between rows

of drying cornstalks, or to slide
into the lullaby of a creek,

my bare skin sinking into cold
mud and slick rock—skin

the color of pearls,
the color of water,
the color of Moon.

MOTHER SEA'S LAMENT

Finless newborn,
you are still three-fourths water
salty as Grandmother Ocean.
Before your first cries rippled air,
your lungs, red-blooming gills,
sifted oxygen from water and blood.
Before your arms flailed against
empty space, they floated, caressed
in my womb's currents. Too soon,
you will begin to dry. While your twin
slips easily between clouds of sunlit
plankton and the enfolding deep, you
will stumble through a desert
of spines and pincers. You'll wake
each morning with sand in your eyes.
Your skin will paper into stiff folds.
Your way will always be unyielding, hard.
Parched winds will blow you far from me.
But trust this:
I keep precious beads of salted water
here in my green eyes, on my slick skin,
in Fallopian cilia, in deep ventricular
channels—beads I drop to guide you
back, to bring you crawling home.

SLIPSTREAM

At 30,000 feet, Indianapolis neighborhoods are
beads strung on white cord, a necklace here,
a bracelet there, a toe ring cul-de-sac. The stepping
stones of factory districts. Off toward Lexington,
the city is a jar of little girls' lightning bugs
that glow and blink. Farther south, forests
are young mens' buzz cuts on this skull of planet,
trimmed around the ears of I-75, clipped
along the neck of the Tennessee River,
smoothed to the chin of the Smokies.
The world is so beautiful, so unimaginable,
it breaks your heart.

A kick in the groin from a bored toddler,
and the scene changes: You're in a living room
of sky, sitting in a recliner teetering on a cloud,
an iPad balanced on your tray table, on which
you write poems of longing, your envy of birds.
A flight attendant rolls a cart past, brings you
water & wine. All around, people unbuckle,
make their way to a bathroom (a bathroom!),
gripe about delays, lost luggage, the tight
squeeze, as they fly, flapless, across a continent.
The world is so beautiful, so unimaginable,
it breaks your heart.

Back home there are dishes and laundry to wash,
in metal boxes that scrub for you, with water
from invisible streams you turn on & off.
You flip through 600 channels of TV,
settle on something you don't watch, white
noise while you check your phone (a computer
in your pocket!) for Facebook goat memes
from that girl you knew in kindergarten.
In twenty minutes, someone you don't know
will bring pre-cooked dinner to your front door.
Remember this: The world is beautiful,
unimaginable. Let your heart break.

TURISTA

Near the Plaza Grande, in la Ciudad Blanca,
Diego sleeps on the curb, propped against
a café gate. In the 120° heat, my helado melts

through its paper cone. Diego shifts, waste-thin,
eyelids twitching in a dream of air conditioning,
carne con papas, baseball cleats.

In his childhood of heat and shade, Diego
wakes each morning, piles into the neighbor's
pickup with five other kids for the long ride

to la Ciudad. They spend the day hustling:
starfish, embroidered dishtowels, meringue
nests—whatever los turistas will buy.

I buy a meringue, give it back to Diego to eat,
buy three more for two sisters and a brother.
My sister, who lives in el centro, keeps granola

bars in her pockets for the kids, wants not to feed
this tidepool of child labor where parents
can't find work, where kids make enough

so at dark when the pickup comes back
for them, families can buy beans and rice.
Later, on the beach at Progreso, we drink

margaritas in the shade. Cruise ships blink
on the horizon. I buy a poem from Eduardo
for $5 US, which he writes on the spot:

> *You are beautiful.*
> *The sun is shining.*
> *Life is beautiful.*
> *Look! The sea is glitter!*

BLUE GARDENIA

In my hair, one blue gardenia,
so she'll recognize me.
Blue gardenias trouble the water

in a cut a crystal bowl
on the altar, each bloom
a burst of blue on the surface

of a small, idyllic sea.
In the air, their bitter perfume
finds me, acid on the tongue,

leaves me speechless, breathless.
She lies pressed in pintucked satin,
Christmas doll new in her package.

One blue gardenia floats in her
hair, blue petals on white satin.
Blue. Blue. Blue. The lid shuts

on her tiny box. Somewhere,
a closing hymn. Blue gardenias
sink below the surface.

NARCISSI

We are spawn of river god x nymph,
you and I. Is it any wonder
we (me) can't see beyond this pool?

Some of us crawl out of the muck
in times of war or famine, but always
we return to our reflections.

Over and over each of us falls in love
with that mythical creation, Self,
with the siren song of our own voice.

We listen not to hear each other,
but for pauses, cracks we can fill
with our own glorious stories.

Kind gestures (we're all about the show)
offer the illusion of kindness,
illuminate our mirrored beauty

in a temporary glow, vanity lights
so everyone, everyone, will look.
Come in close; see how good I am.

We learn too late that like Narcissus,
what we want, we can never have—
to love a reflection we can only

disrupt, to be satisfied with the surface,
to avoid the harder work of looking up,
to be loved in return by these disturbed waters.

ST. ELMO

patron of sailors & the labor of childbirth

Guard my daughter, bobbing
in the salt tide of motherhood,
bait on some god's fine barbed hook,

her dark eyes like black sea stars,
crooked toes trolling murky water,
rosy gills fanning unfamiliar air.

Flush with moon, sea, silver,
she is swollen as a rain-soaked lily.
St. Elmo, you are split open to the sea.

Bless my child with a heart like yours—
pink as coral, strong, buoyant—
as she drifts toward her own child's
salty baptism.

TO MY LGBTQ2, STRAIGHT, AND CORPORATE FRIENDS, IN TERMS OF SEA CREATURES

Like any self-respecting urchin, you bob along with the current,
tube feet fluttering up the sand. You urchins are everywhere, such

comfort in a mob. Almost as an afterthought, you let go your ova
into the brine and go on feeding, no pesky eyes to distract you. The Mr.

rolls past, spills his milt, and you happy couple wish the very best
for little larvae, replicas of urchin lineage unchanged since the Big Bang.

On the other side of the coral bed, you sea cucumbers loll about,
sucking up algae with tube feet modified as mouth parts. You release

ova or sperm. Or, evolutionary geniuses that you are, you save
travel & trouble by doing it all by yourself. You stay safe in your small
    garden.

Drifting in the weeds and muck, insecure urchins turn cucumberphobe.
They roll along in that prickly, swaggery way, spines waving willy-nilly.

They compare spiny shapes or sizes, poison to drive home the point.
Some scared cucumbers, their bodies soft and no legs to run,

self-eviscerate, expel lovely blue filaments, sticky bits of their own
prehensile lungs, to confound hostile urchins. Cucumbers fear urchins.

Urchins spear cucumbers. Brethren echinoderm, if you had brains,
you'd team up, before the indifferent lobster eats you both.

SOUTH DAKOTA WATER: A TRUE LOVE STORY

In South Dakota, we love water not in the way
of a tanned beachgoer on her day off, but
in the way of cacti in rain, storing drops
in convoluted folds behind thorns.

We don't run sprinklers to skip through;
we run them for tomatoes and bush beans,
or trees in midsummer whose fruits we will
put up in fall, so we can eat nostalgia in long winter.

Rivulets fall from gutters not down shiny
brass rain chains, jingling and splashing
on a tiled patio, but into black plastic rain
barrels, keepsafes for the little we can hoard.

In times of drought, we know the correct order:
drinking, dishes, bathing, laundry, from one tin tub
of water. We know to avoid the evaporation
of heating. We know how to be thirsty.

We know water doesn't live in South Dakota.
It passes through, teases and dampens us,
then moves on to Turtle Creek, the James,
the Vermillion, on to the Missouri, the Gulf,
on to places where it can overflow.

PREHENSILE AQUATIC

If only I could breathe
water again, pink gills

fanning in salt soup.
Like mermaids wreathed

in dulse and saw wrack,
I would love the cold,

wish on living stars,
and I too would sing.

You would hear my
liquid lullaby's tremolo

in rock caves or chambered
shells, a song to still

your wringing hands,
soothe your battered,

pounding heart, call you
back to the deep where

we would be weightless
again at last, unborn

in the dark womb
of the sea.

TRITON'S DAUGHTER SNEAKS OUT AT NIGHT

Late one night, you slip your sealskin to feel some real heat, to feel your newly-split legs wrap around a lover's hairless waist, to bear a child or two in a dry bed, to water a garden, eat something cooked and fragrant. Then one day, you're on the beach, marveling at the way water beads on your two thighs, the way your daughter plays with fish in the surf, cupping water and fish in her small, fingered hands, and you hear your father's horn. Quick goodbyes will spare them the tidal wave as you zip back into your sealskin and head out to sea. Your jealous father washes you home.

Another moonlit night, your father is distracted (a new nymph maybe), so you swim back to shore, your fur slick and shedding water. The sea is calm as you make your clumsy way onto land to play with your children. Your son pokes at a fire, your daughter sweeps the doorstep with a handful of beach grass. They talk and laugh as you pull yourself along on clawed flippers, joy trembling in you. But you stop and turn back to the sea, crying in that barking voice of yours, when you see their father step outside in the silver light and shake sand from his bedding—a downy grey sealskin still glistening with saltwater.

WATER TO DUST

From water, dust.
First we are liquid,
blue as an ocean, blue
as bacopia. blue
as a vein, blue as a
stillborn baby.

Then, from a single drop
we gurgle to life,
form ourselves solid
(earth, rock, bone, teeth)
and tightrope time
until there is only

the crumbling body left,
corrupt, dissolving into
blue again, reduced
by time, trouble, joy,
beautiful sorrow.
Into water, dust.

WHAT HE TRIED TO TELL YOU

Sometimes a heart buckles, slows to a *chug chug chug*, the body's pipeline froze up with bad road miles and too many Krispy Kremes. A face goes all bluegrey, the color of sky before winter rain. Skin turns crocodilian, sends all heat to the core. A man drops to his knees. Air thickens to sludge in lungs, so *"Help me"* or *"I love you"* turns from whisper to wheeze. Without his panicky eyes, you'd never hear.

Sometimes you want a cabin on Big Stone Lake, or side chairs made by Amish craftsmen. You want to see the west coast of Wales in autumn. You want a long-haired Chihuahua puppy you can name Leviathan. You want dinner out at Red Lobster, all those boiled claws steaming on your plate. You want to drink the Pinot you were saving, make teenage love on your Amish table, break a lamp or two.

Sometimes, all you want is pink blushing back into pallid skin.

ST. EULALIA of MERIDA
patron of seafarers & mermaids

Mother of Pearl,
ocean's womb of cupped shell,
I am only a grain of sand fallen
from between dragon's teeth,
turned smooth and round,
bleached pale coral, rose pink,
pressed between your ridges,
those delicate finger bones curved
around me, a luminous blind stone.
Release me. Only pulsed out
in a baptismal wash like a dove
from your pink mouth
can I layer on the copper, iron,
muscle & bone to break the surface.
Lift me up to gasp in the thick salt spray,
let me wash up at last
on the rocks.

DROUGHT

Drought on a farm has a way of kicking
the crutches out from under the most
able-bodied, of hobbling the surefooted.

In a drought, raccoons shred
pet peacocks like pulled pork
at Sunday potlucks. Wisteria vines

suck buds back inside, wrens
dump their eggs, bats shrivel
in attic rafters like rows of beef jerky.

The water you spare for tomatoes
attracts desperate badgers, who
drag off whatever poultry and eggs

are left. Bees are long gone. You can
water your brown lawn in the 100-degree
heat, but nothing now will save the chicks—

robin, swallow, mourning dove. The
mother barncat's milk dries up. Ragged
coyotes dig kittens out of straw.

Tucked in your house with your faucets,
you think you're safe. But there's
no rain to fill the aquifers, and Nestle

owns the oceans, bottles the rivers.
Pack away your bone-dry intellect.
Go outside naked. Dance and sing. Pray
for dark skies, for lightning, for water.

TIN GIRL

A plastic coffee mug hangs
from her blue carabiner finger.
Her hair, the color of polished
brass, falls in loose wires
across her face. Her heart
pingpingpings against the steel
bars of her ribs. Her eyes
are two blind rivets. From
the dead slit of her mouth
come grotesque, intermittent
shrieks, singing in the rain.

I want to call out her name,
give her something warm
and dry, a tulip maybe, or
a ripe pear. I want to hold
her until my temporary heat
welds her seamless, until she
dances again. I want to fill her
with helium, make her weightless.
But I'm afraid to move, afraid
even to cry. Look at us—
we're all just rusting machines.

WILD BLUE YONDER

Everyone knows the West begins at Kadoka, South Dakota, where you pull your Volvo into the only gas station, where you end up buying a hunter-orange "Big Cock Country" seed cap, lone strutting pheasant embroidered on the brim, because it will crack up the folks back home. At Wall Drug, mounted jackalopes send fingers of consumer nostalgia up your spine, but you get back on the road. West of the Badlands, you turn ma'am or missy, and tumbleweeds from a cheesy 1950's western finally make it to I-90. They roll toward Mott, North Dakota, where they'll sit a spell, skeletal pom poms fish-hooked on barbed wire. You keep going west, and in the northern Black Hills, things get full-on wild. You turn all bobcat mountain girl, climbing Black Elk Peak with tobacco ties between your teeth, a buck knife in your boot. Did I mention you wear boots now? The Hills spit you out in Wyoming, where you make britches out of antelope hide, start fires with twigs and sinew, hunt jackrabbits and wild plums. There's a hitch in your step now, which makes you veer off. Somewhere north of I-15, Cutbank, Montana let's say, you give up speaking. You strip wires and leather from your Volvo, drive the car into Cutbank Creek. You live in a lean-to made of Russian willow and Volvo leather. You plaster chewed arnica flowers and river mud on a bee sting. You grow a thick white braid overnight, so by morning, it goes all the way down your back. Your bracelets are prairie dog teeth strung on radio wire. You can't remember your name. In a day or a decade, you'll head west again, follow the smell of saltwater.

Back in Sioux Falls, streetlights,
headlights, blue TV lights blink on
like eyes about to cry.

MARCELLA REMUND is a native of Omaha, Nebraska, and a South Dakota transplant, where she teaches at the University of South Dakota in Vermillion. Her poems have appeared in journals including *Pacific Review, Switchgrass Review, The Briar Cliff Review, Amethyst Arsenic, Pasque Petals,* and others, and they have been selected for prizes by judges Odilia Galván Rodríguez and Molly Peacock, by the National Association of State Poetry Societies, and by journal editors. Marcella and her husband live in Vermillion in a multi-generational, multi-species home.

Seamlessly flowing between the glittering oceans of myth and dream and the fossiliz[...] drought-threatened oceans of the high plains, Marcella Remund's *The Sea is My Ugly Tw[...]* conjures up brine-soaked lyrics of elemental transformation, salt, and blood. Part fa[...] tale, part magic spell, part Buddhist koan, part *ecriture feminine*, these deft and haunt[...] poems silkily limn both the beautiful and grotesque with all of the glorious, shape-shifti[...] monstrous seduction of siren song.

      Lee Ann Roripaugh, author of *Dandarians*, South Dakota Poet Laureate

Marcella Remund's *The Sea is my Ugly Twin* is a dreamy collection of "liquid lullabi[...] Playful and surreal, her poems summon our senses to a room that "smells like candles a[...] squid ink," basking us in the pleasures of coffee, seaweed, seal skin and beach grass. W[...] wisdom both earth-bound and crab-like, these poems will bring wry smiles to your l[...] Visit this watery world, shaped by fairytale and myth, today. It will lift you up even a[...] envelops you in its murky depths.

      Christine Stewart, author of *Bluewords Greening* and *Untrussed*

In *The Sea Is My Ugly Twin*, Marcella Remund invites us to disappear. Through ima[...] of otherworldly swells and prehistoric longings, we slide into the sustaining sea, into *Blue. Blue. Blue.* Remund's stunning, evocative lines call us back to where…*we hobbled [...] the shade and made our animal noises.* Such pleasure in this dream of return—even in [...] bodies of *rusting machines* heading West, one more time. A beautiful book.

      Jan Beatty, author of *The Switching/Yard* and *Jackknife: New and Selected Poe[...]*

MARCELLA REMUND is a native of Oma[...] Nebraska, and a South Dakota transplant, where [...] teaches at the University of South Dakota in Vermilli[...] Her poems have appeared in journals including *Pa[...] Review*, *Switchgrass Review*, *The Briar Cliff Rev[...] Amethyst Arsenic*, *Pasque Petals*, and others, [...] they have been selected for prizes by judges Oc[...] Galván Rodríguez and Molly Peacock, by the Natio[...] Association of State Poetry Societies, and by jour[...] editors. Marcella and her husband live in Vermil[...] multi-generational, multi-species home.

ISBN 978-1-63534

$14.99/ POETRY
www.finishinglinepress.com

9 781635 345735

CHANGING MENTAL HEALTH SERVICES

The politics and policy
Tom Butler

CHAPMAN & HALL